GREG NATALE

GREG NATALE
THE LAYERED INTERIOR

FOREWORD BY CLAUD CECIL GURNEY
PHOTOGRAPHY BY ANSON SMART

New York · Paris · London · Milan

CONTENTS

Foreword 7

Introduction 9

Modern Palazzo 17

Perfect Curves 53

Villa Nuova 73

Classic Twist 125

Moody Manor 161

Stepped Stone 197

New Brutalism 233

Deco Dynasty 269

Acknowledgments 285

Sumptuous golden Namban wallpaper by de Gournay as featured in the dining room of the Brisbane River house.

FOREWORD

You only have to flip through the pages of this book to understand why de Gournay and Greg Natale have such an affinity for each other. We love working with Greg as he understands and is passionate about including bold layers of color and painting in his interiors. Gone are the drab beiges and black and whites, and out spring the colorful elements of surprise to grab our attention.

Greg always manages to find the right balance between curves and straight lines; between monochrome and color; between classical and modern; between contemporary and traditional; between art deco and mid-century. His designs are always striking without being over the top, and remain comfortable and livable. I could move into any of his interiors tomorrow.

At every turn, there is an element of surprise—some unusual combinations of materials, with soft fabrics attached to hard metal frames, and then small repeating patterns in soft pastels replaced by huge chunks of primeval colors in the next room. It is difficult to imagine just where Greg goes to in his dreams to produce such imaginative work. I would love to know what he must put into his morning tea or his sundowner.

There is almost the yin and the yang in his designs, with this juxtaposition of hard and soft; of cool and warm; of gloss and matte surfaces; of organic and straight; of zen-like open spaces and laden shelves. It is easy to believe that Greg would have a solution for every space and for the most discerning clients, be it a gypsy caravan or a royal hunting lodge.

Well done, Greg. I love it. Keep it up. Keep surprising us with your creations of art.

CLAUD CECIL GURNEY

The maroon walls of my apartment have inspired a few of my clients. The color brings out the finishes of my vintage, contemporary, and custom pieces, and highlights artworks like this one by Sam Francis.

INTRODUCTION

My mother has a thing about buying property in a valley. She grew up in a two-story house in a Calabrian mountain town and gets claustrophobic when she can't look out over some sort of view. Even our family home in Punchbowl, a thirty-minute drive from Sydney's city center, was situated high enough that we enjoyed a distant view of the Harbour Bridge and the famous New Year's Eve fireworks. I seem to have inherited her fixation with location—every place I've owned has sat on the upper floors of an apartment block or at the high end of a street. So when it came to choosing a location for my flagship store, position was a key factor for consideration.

The story of how I came to open a store in the elegant (and suitably elevated) Sydney suburb of Potts Point has several layers to it, but the first involved good old-fashioned luck. Four years after starting my own business, Greg Natale Design, I was busy creating interiors for a number of residential and commercial projects, focusing on the bold use of color and pattern to craft tailored, sophisticated spaces. The year was 2005, and I attended an event for those in the industry, where I won the lucky door prize: an Arne Jacobsen Egg chair, a Bang & Olufsen hi-fi, and the chance to design a rug that would be produced by leading Australian company Designer Rugs.

Rugs are a passion of mine. They're a great way to introduce color and pattern into a space, to bring balance or contrast, to delineate different areas, and frame a furniture setting. They're one of the important layers that I believe are essential to creating warm, livable interiors, and because I always approach the floors and walls early in a design, they're one of the first pieces I'll consider. After years of trying to find the right rugs for the right spaces, it was a treat to dream up one of my own.

The rug I designed featured my initials as a logo in a repeat geometric pattern (another of my passions). After Designer Rugs made up the rug for me, I embarked on a creative frenzy, producing about forty designs. That first piece had ignited a flame in me that has been burning ever since. What's more, it sparked a conversation with Yosi Tal, managing director of Designer Rugs, about putting together a collection. Never one to let an opportunity slip by, I convinced the company to make up another of my designs, a round rug in a pattern called South Beach, which ended up being featured on the cover of *Belle* magazine in a living setting that, funnily enough, included an Egg chair. After the interest this picture garnered, Designer Rugs agreed to take me on, and my first rug range was born.

The New Regency collection, released in 2009, consisted of six rugs in a variety of colors and geometric designs, inspired by different cities. Everything about this next career step felt right, and even then I could sense that it was the start of something new for me. After the success of that collection, I was approached to create a range of wallpaper for Porter's Paints and, further down the track, a tile collection for Bisazza. Floors and walls—those layers I always begin with—had begun my own journey into product design.

My interior design business continued to grow, as did the opportunities for new collaborations: cushions, furniture, and more rugs, carpets, tiles, and wallpaper. The layers were building. What really gave me the confidence to take the product business further and create my own ranges was opening the new Greg Natale Design headquarters in Surry Hills in 2015. This three-story, split-level building (height again, you see) was inspired by the New York townhouse of fashion designer Halston, which was designed by American modernist architect Paul Rudolph. You couldn't find two greater muses of mine—I have always loved the tailored glamour of Halston's designs, and Rudolph's work with line and form never ceases to amaze me.

A highlight of our headquarters is the boardroom, featuring gray polished plaster walls that recall the predominant hue of Halston's residence. On the floor, my geometric marble tiles in black and white are arranged, almost like a rug, under a Florence Knoll marble-topped table that is surrounded by vintage chairs and lights, a bold, colorful contemporary artwork, and mixed metal accessories. Your office is such an important extension of your brand—it's your aesthetic calling card—and this was worth the years of planning and work. Comfortably settled here, I now had the space to grow my own product range over the following few years. I knew that a flagship store would be the next step, and the design of this boardroom established the blueprint for the store that was to come.

Macleay Street in Potts Point is a beautiful area with a rich architectural heritage, evident in its well-maintained art deco buildings. In 2019, I was lucky to find the perfect spot for my flagship store in one such building, which not only stood at the top of the street but on a street corner—a dream position. Before I could start on the interior design, all my energies went into ensuring that the exterior stylistically reflected its surroundings, anchoring the building within its art deco–era setting. Inspired by the example of local businesses, I worked with a heritage architect to sympathetically recreate the original shop front, from elements such as the front door to materials like the green terrazzo threshold and polished stainless steel trim, which highlights the building's curves.

The interior was easy, starting with gray polished plaster walls and ceilings, and using the same finish on the structural columns in the space. Halston is said to have claimed that everyone looks good in gray, and in the same way I knew this color was the perfect neutral backdrop to showcase my products, regardless of changes in season, style, or collection. Stainless steel and mirrored shelves continue the elegant lines of the store's exterior while keeping the focus on the array of products. But I had to introduce my signature pattern somewhere. Cue the black and white marble floor tiles, featuring the graphic lines of Jurassic black marble, which I also used for the nesting display tables. I don't like to play it safe, and these tiles were as neutral as I could allow while still reflecting my own personality.

For me, an interior design does not work if it's not warm and inviting, and layering is vital to achieving this—it gives a room personality, intimacy, and lasting appeal. In my first book, *The Tailored Interior*, I discussed my approach to building the layers of an interior design—from floors, walls, and ceilings, to window treatments, furniture, and soft furnishings, to accessories and all those finishing touches that I now sell in my store. My design process remains the same, and while trends come and go, I believe the test of a successful interior is the considered application of its layers.

The projects in this book reveal in detail the curated layering of vintage, contemporary, and custom pieces that exemplifies my approach and gives each home its unique personality. They're also testament to the fact that layering extends beyond the tangible, to incorporate heritage, meaning, and the language of design. I invite you to explore these spaces, to immerse yourself in the inspiring photographs, and to read the stories of how they came together. At the time of writing, I'm currently working on my seventh collection for Designer Rugs, checking the latest batch of candles I've created, and thinking up names for a new range of ceramic vases. As with our interiors, it is the many layers that make up our own stories. While I'm still adding more to mine, I'm very grateful for some of its foundations: a little luck, a lot of hard work . . . and a head for heights.

The Arne Jacobsen Egg chair and Bang & Olufsen hi-fi I won, with the first rug I conceived for Designer Rugs. Artwork by Scott Petrie.

OPPOSITE: The boardroom's gray polished plaster walls, marble floor, and metal accents inspired the interior design for my next venture – my flagship store. Artwork by Jo Davenport.

In my store in Sydney's Potts Point, the gray polished plaster walls form a neutral backdrop for the products, which are arrayed on stainless steel and mirrored shelves and marble plinths across a floor of Jurassic marble.

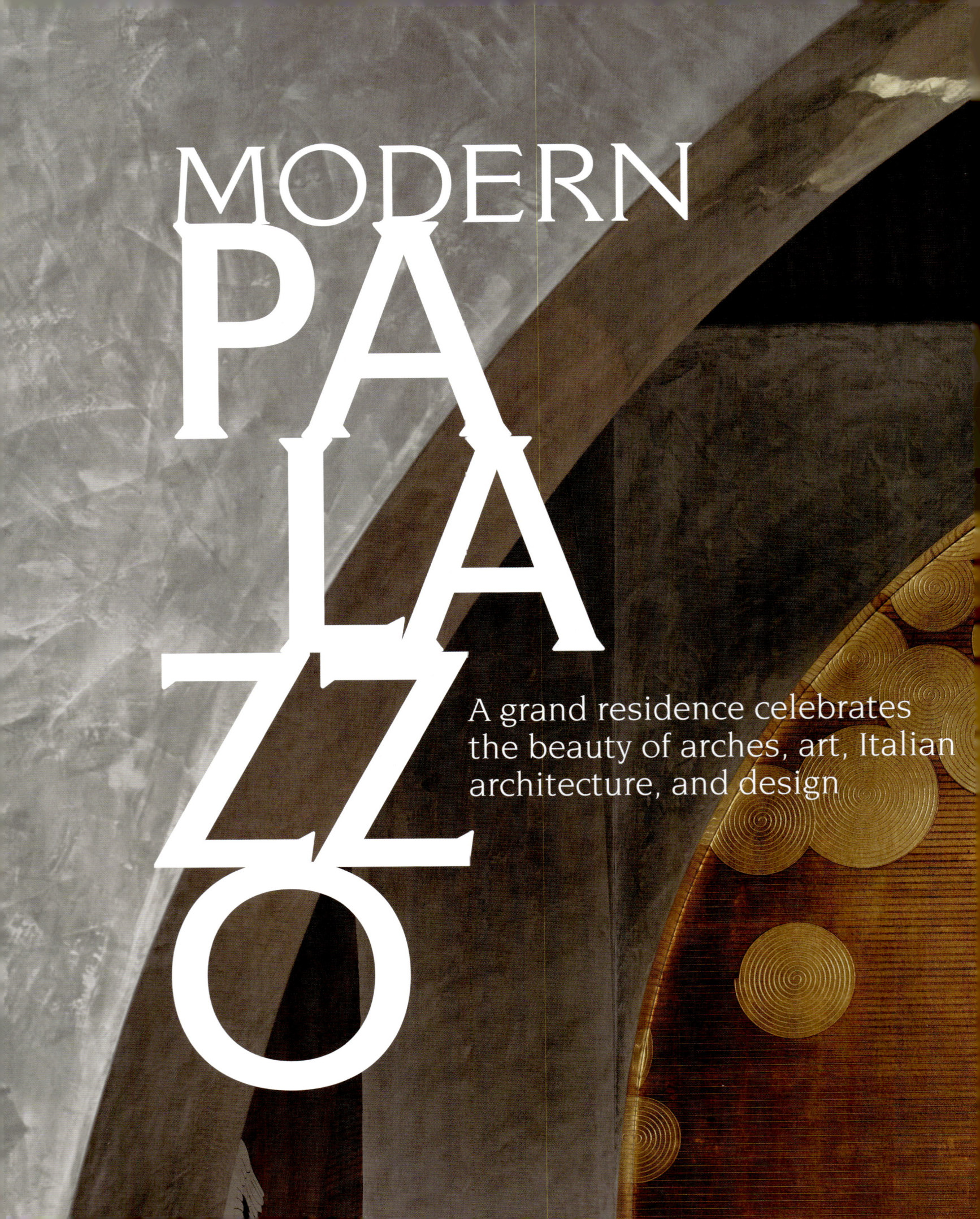

MODERN PALAZZO

A grand residence celebrates the beauty of arches, art, Italian architecture, and design

She gazes out, the perfect arcs of each eye brought into hypnotic focus by their graphic rendering in black and white. Her face, depicted on a pair of cabinets in the entrance to this house, has become an icon due to the obsession of Italian designer Piero Fornasetti. It is a study in classic beauty, the arch of each eyebrow beautifully defined. Yet those arches meet their match in the sculptural curves of architecture that unfurl throughout this striking home.

Italians and arches go way back. The magnificent arcades of the Colosseum, the intersecting arcs of the Pantheon, the baroque dome of Saint Peter's Basilica—these architectural marvels are a proud part of my heritage. Even in suburban Sydney, on the other side of the world, I grew up literally surrounded by arches, as they decorated the exterior and interior of our family house. I love their combination of grace and strength, the openness they give to structures, and the way they allow an appealing flow from one space to the next.

When I undertook the design for this three-story, five-bedroom house on the banks of the Brisbane River in Queensland, the exterior plan already featured a row of arches along its facade. For me, that sparked the concept for an interior showcasing the beauty of arches. The owners, a family with five children, have a love of Italy flowing through their veins. Not only do they have personal ties to Florence but they also run an art school there. I wanted to create a modern palazzo that celebrated their passion for art and all things Italian, using architecture to embrace a classical theme and overlaying it with all the luxuries of contemporary living.

After finessing the exterior layout, I brought the language of those curves into the interior, starting with the entrance. Here, across smooth slabs of Nero Marquina marble, a series of arches begins a story that is told throughout the house's layers. From the interior architecture, which features arches in the hallways, walls, doors, windows, and shelving, the motif extends to the furnishings, with the soft silhouettes of pieces echoing the building's curves. This accumulation of layers, steeped in history but powerful in the present, gives the design its cohesion and impact.

The owners requested a predominantly dark palette, and the marble floors play a significant role here. Laid throughout the house in all-black expanses or paired with white marble in geometric patterns, they make their most dramatic statement at the foot of the staircase. Here, the giant black slabs with their white borders evoke the spirit of grand Italian spaces, while above them the arches begin to take glorious shape. The soaring curves and traversing arcs, the vaulted ceilings and generous walls are all painted in gray velvety stucco, which directs focus toward their pure, classical lines and the intriguing glimpses of other rooms that can be seen between them.

The staircase itself, with its black marble steps, heightens the sense of architectural grandeur, while its sculptural form appears to flow seamlessly into the surrounding stucco walls. The sinuous brass handrail and large pendant light that descends through the void of the staircase bring an opulent gleam that highlights the structure, displaying how drama can come just as much from the lines of architecture as the objects on display.

Brass also features inside the curves of the arches, in the form of delicate finger tiles. Like bands of sunshine, these appear throughout the house, visually marking the shift between certain spaces and materials, as well as bringing a luminosity that offsets the darker tones.

Within the layer of interior architecture are all the intricately curated layers—of furniture and accessories, of color, texture, and detail—that make the space inviting, warm, and livable. Several of the family's own paintings hang on the walls along with artworks they have collected. These are enhanced by the rich hits of color provided by a mix of vintage and contemporary European furniture and a range of patterned wallpaper treatments.

Beyond the stairs, a burst of color seen through the arches announces the dining room, which is swathed in sumptuous de Gournay wallpaper. Against a gold and copper background, white cranes take flight, the sweep of their wings captured within the framing arches of the walls. The warm brick red of velvet chairs resonates above on the red stucco ceiling, in a room that reveals the power of line and form.

From here, various spaces unfold between the curves, including the bar, kitchen, and casual and formal living rooms. Linked by dark fluted timber ceilings, these rooms feature elements that echo the shape of the arches, from the cabinets of the bar to the shades of the pendant light in the kitchen and the rounded backs of the velvet stools below. The brick red color of the stools highlights the gold threads of Paonazzetto marble that forms the countertop and splashback. The treatment of the timber ceiling is repeated in black fluted oak cabinetry below.

Fluting is another layer that appears throughout, its fine, scalloped lines reinterpreting the curve of the arches at an intimate, detailed level. Like the arches, this feature begins at the entrance to the house, in double-height walls of black fluted timber that line a glass-fronted atrium. The light-filled structure provides a modernist element that connects to the black brick exterior while suggesting the grand proportions of the spaces to follow.

Inside, black fluted timber walls and a fluted marble fireplace make a statement in the formal living room, where furniture in tones of brick and mustard continues the vibrant look of the adjacent dining room. In the pool room downstairs, where the mood, furnishings, and colors are lighter, the fluted ceiling is painted white and the walls covered with foliage, courtesy of green and lemon Fornasetti wallpaper.

Fluting also brings exquisite detail to the spa, where a fluted marble bath looks like a small-scale architectural structure in itself, flanked by fluted gray finger tiles and glass shower screens. The use of monochromes in this area is softened by brass accents like arched doors on the vanities, luxe finishes such as ombré glass mosaic tiles on the steam room walls, and surprising touches like quirky fish on the wallpaper of the powder room.

Wallpaper presents a dynamic way of bringing color, pattern, and wit to various rooms. One charming floral motif appears in different colorways between bedrooms, giving each its own distinct personality. In another bedroom, Fornasetti wallpaper delivers a playful take on the iconic arched facades of buildings in Saint Mark's Square, Venice. Again, the layers of architecture, culture, and decorative detail are interwoven to great effect.

After the cranes of the dining room, birds reappear on the serene mint-colored Gucci wallpaper of the master bedroom. The elegant lines of the herons' long necks draw the eye from every angle and echo the curves of the scalloped ceiling, while the warm russet tones of their heads are picked up in the velvet bed, bench, and curtains.

Arches resume their story in this room, from the curve of the bedhead to the recessed shelves, steel-framed windows, and doorways that lead to the adjoining ensuite and make-up area. Here, gray fabric wallpaper provides a textural background to the gray marble bath and the black vanities. Brass accents—in the arched mirrors, details, and finger tiles—highlight the shapes, turning these rooms into a symphony of curves.

Back at the entrance, that first series of arches commands attention in the shifting light, especially when viewed through the fluted glass of the atrium. By day, the space floods the arches with sunlight; at night, it reveals them basking in the glow of the brass tiles, under the iconic gaze of a watchful eye, in a place that blends classic forms and contemporary style.

Light flooding into the house's entrance lands on the striking details of the black fluted timber walls and black and white marble floor. A selection of vintage, contemporary, and custom furniture throughout the house includes a pair of Fornasetti cabinets. Artworks by Antonia Mrljak add another dramatic layer to the entrance spaces.

A series of sweeping arches can be seen from the staircase, their generous curves highlighted by the gray stucco finish. Glimpses of the dining and formal living rooms appear through the curves.

A grand room for a grand piano.

OPPOSITE: The vibrant brick red of Eero Saarinen velvet chairs and the stucco ceiling provide a rich contrast to beautiful golden de Gournay wallpaper in the dining room.

In the formal living room, mustard and brick tones continue the palette under a black fluted timber ceiling. Brass-lined shelves full of accessories provide another opulent layer.

Black timber fluting in the kitchen offsets the gold veins of Paonazzetto marble. Verner Panton velvet stools offer another burst of color in a room that celebrates the beauty of its materials.

The elegant brass finger tiles that line the arches combine with the silky stucco walls to create a luminous effect.

OPPOSITE: Timber fluted ceilings and Nero Marquina marble floors link the casual living room and bar to the kitchen.

Upstairs, brass-lined arches establish a glamorous mood in the make-up area off the master bedroom, with the black marble bath in the ensuite lying beyond.

OPPOSITE: The dressing room features the same dramatically scalloped ceiling as the master bedroom.

Serene mint green provides the backdrop for the master bedroom in the form of Gucci Heron wallpaper. The arched bedhead continues the play on curves, while warm brick tones connect this space to the downstairs decor.

A palette of neutral hues works with the foliage of Fornasetti wallpaper in another bedroom. The wallpaper appears in a few different colorways between rooms.

More wonderful arches in the wallpaper set the scene for a bedroom of rosy hues. I wanted each bedroom to have its own personality.

OPPOSITE: Another bedroom uses the foliage wallpaper in a deeper tone. Doors and windows continue the language of arches.

On the lowest floor, a home theater beckons in sophisticated hues.

OPPOSITE: My custom art deco–inspired rugs bring another layer of color, pattern, and warmth to the house. The staircase unfurls to end in this vignette with a vintage burl and brass table from Florence.

The spa area reveals an attractive blend of finishes, with delicate gray finger tiles, gray terrazzo, a fluted marble bath, and geometric-patterned floor tiles.

OPPOSITE: My gray mosaic tiles in an ombré effect create a sense of enveloping luxury on the walls of the steam room.

Wallpaper brings a little whimsy to the powder room, while the arched brass cabinet doors add drama.

OPPOSITE: Pastel tones grace the guest bedroom, courtesy of another decorative wallpaper.

The furnishings of the pool room are lighter, with mustard and mint tones creating a fresh mood beneath a white timber fluted ceiling. Seating by GamFratesi for Gebrüder Thonet is arranged over a vintage Moroccan rug.

The exterior arches were my starting point for the design.

OPPOSITE: An outdoor terrace setting on my Corsica tiles looks out on the serene view of the Brisbane River.

PERFECT CURVES

Soft, feminine contours and colors transform a harborside penthouse

Viewed from above, the vignette is a mesmerizing one. A luxurious rug draws the eye, with its pattern of concentric circles in tones of pink, gray, and yellow. Around it, an invitingly curved sofa and armchair in gray bouclé fabric face another softly curved chair in caramel velvet. In the middle sits a coffee table and, toward the edge, a side table, their circular forms making them appear like tiny planets orbiting the rug's pastel planes. All have organic lines and rounded silhouettes, in a setting that is central—both physically and aesthetically—to the home's design.

The soft and feminine poetry of curves was at the heart of the brief for this two-story, three-bedroom apartment in the Sydney harborside suburb of Walsh Bay. Located beside one of the city's most iconic curved structures, the Sydney Harbour Bridge, this sunny penthouse is part of a striking modern building in a heritage area. The owners wanted a bright contemporary space for themselves and their two sons, and a sophisticated play on curves winds its way through every layer of the design, from interior architecture to furnishings, accessories, even artworks. With white walls and ceilings throughout, the focus is on the fluid lines of the architecture and how they define and connect different spaces, echoed by the complementary forms of modern European furniture.

For me, the beauty of curvilinear design is that it offers a chance to express movement, energy, and sculptural beauty in an interior and honor its simple, clean lines.

That striking circular rug with its elegant grouping of pieces sits in the living area, a serene, light-filled oasis with a double-height void above that allows the curves to make a powerful statement. The generosity of the void brought with it a sense of openness and connectivity between spaces, which I wanted to enhance and emphasize.

My design for the apartment's renovation began with the resizing, reconfiguring, and even relocating of spaces to align better with the void.

The most significant shift was the staircase, which was moved from an awkward spot in the middle of the apartment to the end of the living area. Now, it gracefully climbs one side of the void, its smooth white wall merging into the larger expanse of walls behind. The staircase flows in rhythm with other structural curves that have been integrated into the walls, namely the new fireplace and, below that, a built-in bench with cabinetry that wraps around the room.

The effect is wonderfully enveloping, where the seamless, almost amorphous forms of the interior architecture are highlighted by the all-white finish. In harmony with this, the gray Carrara marble of the benchtop, fireplace, and door reveal presents a gentle shift in tone. Solid oak floorboards bring textural contrast and link the living, dining, and kitchen areas, which flow into one another in the open-plan space beneath the void. Laid in a chevron pattern, the floorboards also provide added detail, while their blond color works with the other hues in the room to bring warmth to the space.

If curves are one integral element articulated through the layers of the interior, palette is another. Among all the white surfaces, the owners requested a color scheme of pink, gray, and yellow. These feminine hues suit the sensual, organic lines of both architecture and furniture, merging with the curves to make an impact that is softly toned yet substantial.

While the circular rug in the living area captures the apartment's palette in one luxurious layer, the curvaceous bouclé sofa and armchair offer a cocooning retreat in gray. Opposite, the caramel velvet armchair beckons, while its fabric reappears in the nearby velvet dining chairs, which are arrayed in a mix of natural and blush tones. The shape of the chairs and the oak dining table continue the language of curves, bringing a cohesive look to the adjacent living and dining spaces.

In the kitchen beyond, rounded yellow leather stools deliver a bolder burst of color. Here, too, curves are a feature, chiefly in the island, which has a hand-carved cylindrical base. With both island and splashback in gray Carrara marble and the cabinetry in white, decorative elements are minimal here, allowing line and form to speak for themselves. The brass of the stool legs, light fitting, and tapware introduces another element that recurs in accents throughout the apartment, bringing a warm gleam to the delicate palette.

Upstairs, the layering of curves begins again with the fluid lines of interior architecture. In this case, the ceiling sets the scene in the master bedroom, a large open-plan space that encompasses a bedroom, walk-in robe, ensuite, and sitting area. With no cornices or walls to interrupt the flow, the molded form of the coffered ceiling snakes its way around the room, creating a subtle delineation of areas. Nowhere is this more effective than in the ensuite, where the placement of gray Carrara marble floor tiles mirrors the shape of the ceiling. The rounded edge of those tiles, surrounded by blond oak floorboards, highlights the allure of this space as another little oasis in the apartment, made even more special by the beautiful finishes.

A white freestanding bath and sculptural side table bring their own seductive curves to the setting, echoed by the shapes of the circular sinks and spherical wall sconces. The smallest heroes of the space are the white mosaic finger tiles on the wall, which hug its curves, drawing attention to them while delivering a lovely intricacy of detail. Offsetting the white and gray finishes, brass tapware and accents continue to provide warmth and glamour, with a brass skirting trim adding a defining line around all the areas here, as it does downstairs.

The owners wanted a master bedroom and ensuite that had all

the luxury and style of a hotel suite, and the materials and palette work with the curves to achieve this. In the sitting area, a pink velvet sofa creates a beautiful arc with its form, teamed with divinely soft white lambswool chairs. With a cluster of orb-like lights and a rounded glass table, the scene is reminiscent of the living space downstairs, although here the patterned rug of pink, gray, and yellow reveals more angles in contrast. Following the contours of the ceiling around the space, the next area is the bedroom, which continues the palette, after which the walk-in wardrobe begins, with custom cabinetry in limed oak and a little integrated curved table.

Other rooms in the apartment continue the play on curves in varying degrees, with white mosaic finger tiles again emphasizing the rounded walls of the powder room. In this room, the asymmetry of the organic-shaped mirror and angular gray and white marble vanity adds an element of surprise, as well as a sense of movement that balances the smaller space. In the boys' bathroom, the finger tiles are gray, creating a tonal blend with the Carrara marble floors and long vanities. While the boys' bedrooms expand the apartment's palette, introducing tones of dark blue and pale green, the treatment of these colors is understated, and curves still make their mark in the integrated bedhead cabinetry and the furniture.

From the robust form of an ottoman to the dome of a bedside lamp, the layering of curves continues, extending even to the brushstrokes on canvas, with some artworks featuring organic splashes and others more defined arcs. Amid the liberating flow of connected spaces, there is a sense that all the apartment's lines weave their way back to the living area, where the family congregates and the design's heartbeat begins. Here is a space shaped by its curves, where you can see layering create its own language of line to express a home's character, from the surface of a wall to the circles on a rug.

In the living area, the concentric circles of my rug act as an anchor for the grouping of furniture on it.

OPPOSITE: Beneath a pink-hued artwork at the entrance, a pair of lamps and a bench by GamFratesi for Gebrüder Thonet begin the play on curves.

The inviting organic forms of two Tacchini sofas in gray bouclé offer a cocooning retreat in the living area, which features artworks by Diana Miller (left) and Kate Banazi (right).

Gubi velvet chairs in natural and blush shades bring more curves to the mix, while an artwork by Simon Barlow adds a soft touch.

OPPOSITE: Yellow leather stools provide a pop of color in the kitchen, while the hand-carved Carrara marble base of the island makes it a feature.

White finger tiles hug the curved walls of the powder room, with an asymmetrical mirror and marble vanity providing elements of surprise.

OPPOSITE: Beneath a Claire Kirkup artwork, a Gubi sofa and Baxter chairs create a luxurious layout in the sitting area off the master bedroom.

The master bedroom continues the feminine palette, with the language of curves picked up in an artwork by Leonie Barton.

OPPOSITE: Gently framing the room with its contours, the coffered ceiling mirrors the lines of the marble floor to delineate the ensuite in this space. The sculptural bath and side table define this as a special sanctuary.

More finger tiles emphasize the curved walls of the other bathroom, which features a tonal blend of cool grays.

OPPOSITE: In another bedroom, the palette shifts to pale green, but curves remain in the ottoman and timber bedhead.

Lightweight outdoor furniture on the balcony keeps the focus on the view, where the iconic curves of the Sydney Harbour Bridge provide a stunning backdrop.

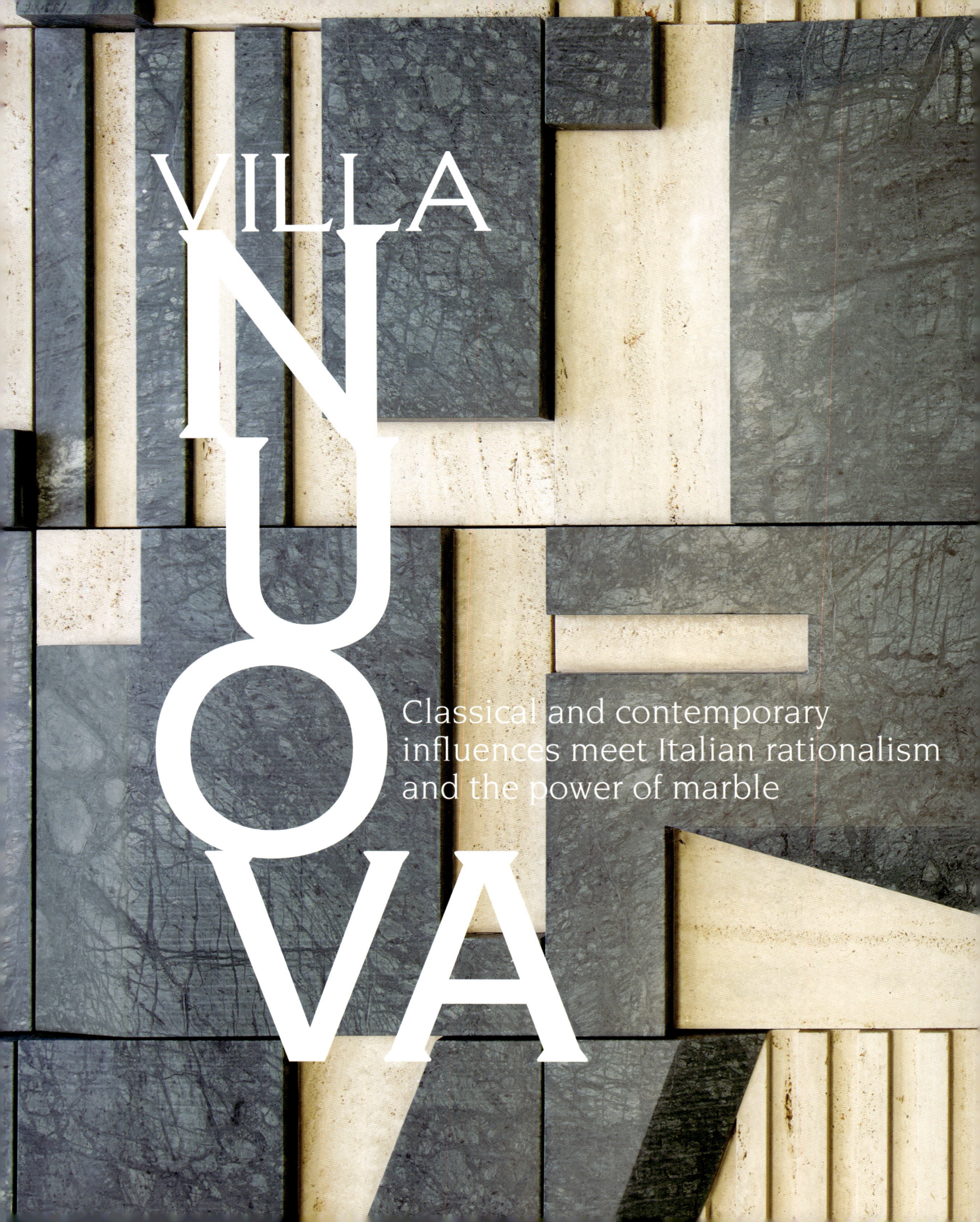

VILLA NUOVA

Classical and contemporary influences meet Italian rationalism and the power of marble

The language of interior design has many layers. We talk a lot about furniture and accessories—the sofas we sit on, the cushions we sink into, the ornaments we choose to inject our personal style. But so much of a house's character comes from the interior architecture—the floors under our feet, the walls that surround us, the hallways we traverse, the portals and doors we walk through. These different framing elements and the intriguing spaces in between have much to say, and their materiality can define the narrative of a house.

When you step through the oversized bronze doors of this remarkable contemporary villa in the harborside Sydney suburb of Mosman, you experience a moment that encapsulates the essence of the design in more ways than one. First, there are the floor tiles. Outside the doors, large slabs of marble in shades of burgundy, pink, and ivory are laid in a classical Palladiana mosaic style. Inside, the combination of marble tiles shifts to a geometric pattern of burgundy, pink, green, and ivory. Those four colors set the scene for the palette of the four-story, five-bedroom house, and marble plays a significant role throughout as one of its most expressive materials.

But there is more at play in this vignette. The pattern of the interior tiles reveals an art deco influence, which continues in the triangular fluting on the timber walls. Then there is the brutalist style of the glass mirror hanging on one wall. And lastly there are those statement doors with their large bronze and glass panels, inspired by Italian rationalism.

These three styles were my main influences for the design of this grand house. How they came to work together was a response to the structure of the building itself, the owners' brief, and my European sojourns.

Travel is always a doorway to fresh inspiration, and prior to this project I was fortunate to have enjoyed several trips to Italy and France. One of the most significant experiences for me was visiting Milan's Villa Necchi Campiglio, built in the 1930s at the height of the Italian rationalist movement. I fell in love with its blend of pared-back classicism and modernity, and the beauty of its marble and granite floors and portals, timber-paneled walls, and metal doors.

Those features came to mind when I began the interior design of this house, which centered on merging the classical and the contemporary. The building may have been modern but still had elements like a pitched roof and eaves, and rather than a minimalist style the owners wanted some traditional attributes like cornices and a design full of warm tones. He had a fondness for art deco, she liked late 1970s furniture, and both requested blond oak floors. My travels in Paris led me to incorporate the chevron pattern of the floorboards that appear in some bedrooms and living areas.

But it was the introduction of marble and granite that unifies the design of this house. Modern builds can be blank canvases and all-white spaces can overwhelm, especially in large rooms. To me, the unique colors and patterns of stone not only help to break up those spaces and add detail and warmth, but they also bring their own sense of history. In a "forever" house like this, for the couple and their two older children who come to stay on and off, the marble and granite in the floors, walls, portals, and furniture create a new design history, layering the classical over the modern. The fact that there are twenty-eight different types of stone in this house makes that history more interesting.

With the view of the sparkling harbor beyond, the huge open-plan living, sitting, and dining area owes its sense of grandeur to the granite that defines the spaces.

In generous strips that run along the floorboards and up the walls, in substantial beams that wrap around white lacquered ceilings, its gray, ivory, and black veins provide a beautifully decorative frame. Within that, the palette is made up of neutrals, gold, and white in shapely pieces that range from the curve of a cream wool sofa to the solidity of a brass brutalist chair. Artworks at each end of the space echo the lines of the granite and create their own dialogue with the furniture in the room, which is a mix of vintage, contemporary, and custom designs.

In the adjacent kitchen, under a pink Murano pendant light, 1970s touches appear in the metal stripes of the island cabinetry and the pantry with its square timber paneling, a finish that features on cabinetry in the house. These brutalist elements take their cue from a courtyard at the center of the house, surrounded by bronze-framed glass windows and spanning two floors. To amplify the silhouette of a Japanese maple tree in the courtyard, I designed a sculpture on the wall behind, using fluted travertine panels overlaid with a form in green marble that suggests the tree's shadow. The delicate old tree and the bold new sculpture make a powerful pairing.

A spiral staircase continues the neutral palette with its ivory marble steps and fluted timber walls, while the pink accents that appear upstairs begin here, in a stunning quartz pendant light. On the first floor, the bedrooms, ensuites, and study zones are arrayed around the courtyard, linked by timber fluting on the ceiling. The master bedroom and ensuite, situated above the living area and enjoying that same incredible view, are serene spaces that are rich in materiality yet still restrained in style. In the bedroom, beige leather-paneled walls offer a luxurious setting, with marble featuring in the bedhead, bedside tables, skirting, and trim.

Pink tones appear in the furnishings, lights, and art deco–inspired rug, while the pinky gray lines of Volakas marble in the ensuite create a striking display. The influence of Italy returns in the gray terrazzo floor—lined, Villa Necchi–style, with strips of marble—and in the sculptural 1970s look of the custom bath, which was inspired by street furniture I saw in southern Italy. Again, classical and contemporary combine to great effect.

The rich burgundy and green of the marble entrance tiles play their part on the lower floors. In the family room near the front door, burgundy marble walls melt into a stucco ceiling to create a moody space that is intensified by black-stained floors, a black sofa and light, and a vintage brass console. Burgundy continues on the floor below in a series of rooms that form their own apartment within the house. Here, across the same Palladiana tiles of the entrance, the rich red hue appears in a velvet sofa and a marble bar, even extending to a marble barbecue on the terrace outside. The scheme is lightened by vast white coffered ceilings, a feature that I integrated throughout the house to increase the sense of height and drama.

Green marble makes its mark on the next floor down, in a different arrangement of Palladiana tiles but also in the portals of a mesmerizing tunnel that leads from the house's other entrance to the garage. That lush mossy green was inspired by the couple's Aston Martin cars and, accompanied by fluted timber walls, brings another sophisticated layer to the design.

A final glimpse of the house through its rear door sees another defining moment. The same bronze and glass used for the front entrance open onto that lovely green marble of the floor and walls, while a set of stairs leads up to the pool. The stairs are paved in Roman bricks, a favorite of modernist architect Frank Lloyd Wright, which I saw in his famous Robie House in Chicago. Another trip, another inspiration, but still with a little Italy at its heart, drawing classicism and modernism together with love.

Palladiana mosaic-style tiles begin the story of marble that gives this house much of its character.

OPPOSITE: The imposing bronze and glass front doors were inspired by my visit to the Villa Necchi Campiglio in Milan, an icon of 1930s Italian rationalism.

The powder room combines the deep burgundy marble floor with the soft pink of my moiré mosaic tiles. The vanity's brutalist-style timber paneling appears throughout the house.

OPPOSITE: At the entrance, an Italian brutalist mirror sits above a cane-leg console. The geometric floor tiles establish the palette for the house's use of marble.

In the family room, Rosso Levanto marble walls and a stucco ceiling in the same burgundy hue provide an opulent backdrop. I created the coffered ceiling to make space for the contemporary pendant light and stained the floorboards black for added impact.

OPPOSITE: A vintage 1970s lamp and chair and a custom console make an evocative grouping in one corner of the room.

A brass and resin coffee table adds its unusual lines to the gold tones of my custom rug.

OPPOSITE: The red glass frame of a 1970s Italian mirror, which sits above a brutalist brass console, was the starting point for the richly hued scheme.

The light-filled courtyard at the center of the house features my brutalist sculpture in fluted travertine and green marble.

OPPOSITE: The bronze and glass front doors, the art deco-inspired patterned floor tiles, the fluted timber paneling—these materials encapsulate the house's blend of materiality and styles.

Encased by gray, ivory, and black veins of granite, the formal living area presents a sumptuous mix of neutral tones and brass accents. A pair of bronze sculptures by Stephen Ormandy frames and complements the view of the courtyard beyond.

The warm tones of the kitchen cabinetry highlight details such as the 1970s-style metal stripes of the island and the pantry's bold timber paneling.

OPPOSITE: In the sitting area, Parisian cabinets echo the abstract lines of a Dale Frank painting.

An artwork by Antonia Mrljak offers another harmonious response to the room's granite framework, with subtly patterned wallpaper behind. A pair of Gio Ponti lamps and the monolithic legs of my custom table anchor the dining setting with their iconic forms.

A pink quartz pendant light by Christopher Boots adorns the spiral staircase with its fluted timber walls.

OPPOSITE: More Palladiana tiles pave the way for a beautiful setting outside the open-plan living, sitting, and dining area.

The pink tones of the upstairs areas appear in a pair of contemporary artworks on the landing and in a runner that is Palladiana-like in its design.

OPPOSITE: The art deco motif of the lift doors is in keeping with the house's stylistic influences.

Timber adds its warmth to the brick and pink hues of upstairs study zones, with marble skirting and trim maintaining a link with other areas of the house.

A vintage Vladimir Kagan chair in its original upholstery is a stylish place to enjoy the view in the master bedroom.

OPPOSITE: The bedhead's marble inlay forms a beautiful curve on the leather-paneled walls with their small brutalist pattern.

The planes of marble and the white lacquered ceiling pick up the light that flows into the master walk-in robe.

OPPOSITE: In the master ensuite, the sculptural shape of the bath presents a strong contrast to the lines of Volakas marble on the walls and the terrazzo and marble floors.

The pinkish golden vein of Calacatta Viola marble works with the fluted timber ceiling and brutalist-style vanity in another ensuite.

OPPOSITE: In this bedroom, de Gournay wallpaper delivers a pattern of soft ripples in neutral tones for a textural look.

Another bedroom sees brick-colored accents bring a sophisticated look to the neutral palette. The shagreen panels and aged brass frame of the wardrobe add a further luxurious touch with their finishes.

In the lower ground-floor hallway, art deco–inspired geometric tiles complement the lines of a custom mirror by Hava Studio.

OPPOSITE: The ceiling's timber fluting forms an attractive corner feature above an artwork by Suzy O'Rourke.

Rosso Levanto marble comes into its own in the bar area on the lower floor. I created exaggerated coffered ceilings in this zone to enhance the height of the rooms and add drama.

OPPOSITE: An artwork by Bec Smith highlights the curves and color of a burgundy velvet sofa in the style of Jean Royère.

In the lower guest bedroom, de Gournay wallpaper provides a soft backdrop for the darker tones, which take their cue from an Antonia Mrljak painting. A pink Cassina chair and moiré curtains balance the black vintage 1970s lamps and brutalist-style bedside tables.

Calacatta Viola marble adds its blend of wine-red tones to the guest ensuite, with another timber-paneled vanity at the center.

OPPOSITE: A brutalist-patterned timber ceiling presides over the lower outdoor dining area, with its barbecue in burgundy marble.

The pool, framed in my mosaic tiles from Bisazza, enjoys a spectacular view at all times of day.

A timber-paneled cabinet in a brutalist style adds to the pattern play at this rear entrance to the house.

OPPOSITE: The deep mossy green of Verde Guatemala marble defines the garage level in more Palladiana floor tiles and in the portals of the fluted timber hallway.

The couple's cars were my inspiration for the use of green marble in the lowest level of the house. Located at the end of that long, theatrical hallway, I like to think of this garage area, with its green terrazzo floor, as their own little "Batcave."

The back view of the house presents another strong blend of materials, with exterior sandstone walls and a copper garage door.

OPPOSITE: The rear door, in the same bronze and glass paneling as the front entrance, opens onto that lovely green marble and a staircase of Roman bricks that leads up to the pool area.

CLASSIC TWIST

Old and new combine with French flair to revitalize a Victorian mansion

In the entrance hallway of this magnificent house, two forms sit side by side on the white walls. They couldn't be further apart in style and era, yet they seem to share a connection. One, a sculpture by contemporary Australian artist Anya Pesce, is a sheet of molded plastic that twists, ribbon-like, down the surface of the wall. The other is the corbel at the base of the hallway's arch, one of many decorative architectural elements in the house, which was built in 1885. Although an unexpected pairing, their shapes speak to each other eloquently in the space while encapsulating the dual language of the house, where the contemporary is layered over the traditional.

The suburb of Ashfield in Sydney's inner west is home to several impressive Victorian-era residences. When I was a child, driving around the city with my parents, I'd gaze at them in wonder from the back seat of the car, admiring the filigree-style architecture with its cast-iron "lace" verandas. Back then, I always wished I could step inside one of the houses and take a look around. Once I'd chosen my career path, I wished not only to step inside one but also to design its interior.

Having bought this two-story, four-bedroom house for themselves and their three young sons, the owners wanted to transform the place to suit their modern lifestyle. The house had undergone a renovation in the 1980s that had updated some areas but left several poky little rooms, and both its exterior and interior appeared to be weighed down under a heavy color scheme of burgundy and yellow.

While I love the considered use of color in a house's design, I believed this historic building required the classic combination of black and white to refresh its look and bring out its beauty. The white exterior and interior now present an elegant contrast to the black iron balustrades and brackets on the verandas, and black timber balustrades on the stairs inside. New black-stained oak floorboards laid in a chevron pattern provide depth and interest, while French paneling is one of the most significant additions to the interior architecture. I introduced this to add texture and detail to the walls, as well as in response to the era of the house.

One of the owners has a love of all things French, and there is something about Victorian houses that lend themselves to the style of nineteenth-century Parisian apartments. With that in mind, I began the interior design, moving from the paneling and parquetry floors to a focus on introducing contemporary layers of joinery and furniture that would bring a lighter feel to the traditional structure. After staining a couple of the owners' existing pieces of French furniture black, I brought in designs with a midcentury inspiration.

The front rooms of the house are moody spaces with walls painted inky blue, an evocative shade that delivers a little drama and offsets the gray marble of the original fireplaces. Furniture in dark gray or deep blue channels a midcentury look, with rugs adding geometric patterns and custom cabinets bringing contemporary character and the gleam of brass. In the media room, bookshelves feature ladders hanging from brass rails; in the games room, a bar cabinet is the picture of Parisian style with brass mesh doors and mirror-backed shelves.

Across the hallway, a lighter shade of blue sets a more relaxed tone for the boys' rumpus room, but common to all three areas is the treatment of the cornices, which are painted the same color as the walls. With the ceilings remaining white, this element modernizes and lifts the traditionally formal spaces.

If blues envelop the front areas of the house, pink tones warm its back rooms, where the interiors have a stronger connection to the outside, and a lighter palette prevails. A long art deco–inspired runner leads along the entrance hallway to the kitchen, living, and dining areas, where I opened up walls to eliminate the smaller rooms and created large, open spaces more in harmony with the family's lifestyle. The runner's hues of blush and gray announce the palette that connects these areas, which are also punctuated by brass accents.

A grouping of blush dining chairs echoes the color of the sheer curtain in the kitchen, providing a delicate balance to the large gray marble island. Here, an integrated second slab of marble forms an extended dining area to create one monolithic sculptural piece that makes a striking modern statement in the room. The rounded chairs and the clusters of white spheres in the pendant lights soften the space, while brass-framed cabinets with fluted glass appear more like freestanding furniture pieces than built-in cupboards. With sunshine flooding in from the new white timber-framed French doors, the room is chic and welcoming.

Soft blush tones continue in the living and dining areas, where the curvaceous forms of furniture enhance their feminine appeal. In the living room, two rounded sofas, one in gray, the other in a neutral pattern, sit opposite pale pink armchairs, with a midcentury coffee table and a brass étagère lending their own curves to the scene. In the dining room, around the owners' black-stained French table, the organic forms of 1950s-style blush velvet chairs make an attractive picture. Sheer curtains in the same tone provide a further link between the rooms, as do a pair of my rugs featuring the same palette in an abstract pattern.

Beyond these spaces you can see curves appear in the arched doors of a nearby pavilion, which was built for the many family and children's parties that the owners host. The space contains a pizza oven, barbecue, and large dining table on a floor of black and white marble tiles. On the vast 25,000-square-foot property, this generous addition remains sympathetic to the house's design, another contemporary layer that engages with and enhances the traditional.

Before the stairs is the powder room, a richly hued space like a little jewel, featuring chinoiserie wallpaper in serene pale green. The brick color of the curtains and the brass-framed mirror add dramatic touches, balanced by soft gray marble tiles, while the clean lines of the marble vanity bring a modern edge.

My carpet in gray and taupe covers the upstairs areas, the style of which is reminiscent of the late designer David Nightingale Hicks, a long-time influence of mine. I believe it is the layering of finishes that achieves this—the geometric motif of the carpet, the mélange of modern furniture and traditional architecture, the feather-patterned curtains and Roman blinds, and the panels of blush-colored wallpaper.

These last transform the walls of the master suite, in grassweave fabric that provides a beautifully textural effect between the crisp white moldings. Another series of interconnected spaces that I opened up in the house's redesign, this area features furniture in the same delicate palette as the downstairs living areas, from gray chaises to a curvy velvet blush ottoman, which offsets the lines of a midcentury-style four-poster bed. The ensuite continues with gray in the marble countertop, ceiling-high splashback, and patterned tiles, while more chinoiserie wallpaper brings softly contrasting colors.

On this floor, blue and gray resume their deeper notes in the boys' bedrooms and ensuites, in another link to the palette downstairs. Here, finishes such as bronze corners on navy custom cabinetry, geometric-patterned floor tiles, subway wall tiles in white or navy, and fluted glass all deliver further detail.

This grand house is a lifelong project for the family, which will continue to evolve with their lifestyle. The next plan is for a conservatory on the grounds—another old-world element that will be imbued with new features to join the layered language of tradition and modernity.

A white molded plastic sculpture by Anya Pesce and a glossy black Wiggle bench by Paul Wells from Becker Minty bring contemporary lines to the hallway's classic architecture.

OPPOSITE: The house's elegant black and white exterior highlights its grand proportions and filigree details.

Shades of inky blue and gray give a sophisticated feel to the games room, which features midcentury-style furniture.

OPPOSITE: Brass mesh doors and mirror-backed shelves elevate the bar cabinet with their burnished gleam.

In the boys' rumpus room, featuring an artwork by Andrew Bennett, a lighter shade of blue on the walls denotes a change of pace.

OPPOSITE: Beneath an artwork by Mel Brigg in the media room, a gray Milo Baughman sofa complements the angles of my Dunand rug.

The kitchen island of Volakas marble, with its extended slab for dining, makes a strong sculptural statement that is offset by blush-hued chairs and delicate brass-framed cabinets.

Two of my Onyx rugs link the adjacent dining and living areas, where a palette of blush and gray prevails. In the living room, seating by Kelly Wearstler brings an inviting series of curves.

The doors of the newly built pavilion continue the arched motif that runs through the house's interior architecture.

The owners' French commode, now stained black, sits on my Geo Deco runner in the hallway, near an artwork by Elsbeth Shaw.

OPPOSITE: In the powder room, brass accents and marble add elegant layers to the beautiful backdrop of chinoiserie wallpaper.

My Yves carpet in gray and taupe provides a subtly detailed neutral layer for furniture in the upstairs hallway, including a vintage-style bench seat upholstered in my Scala fabric, which picks up the pink tones of an artwork by Claire Kirkup.

Blush-colored grassweave wallpaper in the master bedroom offers a textural, cocooning effect between the white moldings, with a four-poster bed of black cerused oak delivering bold lines amid the softly hued scheme.

The delicate details of the ensuite's chinoiserie wallpaper works with the striking gray slabs of Volakas marble and my Ponti marble floor tiles.

The walk-in robe features a pretty fringed gray ottoman.

OPPOSITE: Above a tiered cabinet, an artwork by Ash Holmes deepens the tonal blend of the master bedroom.

Blush-painted walls and cabinetry make this upstairs study an appealing area. A sculpture by Jean Paul Mangin plays on the house's brass accents, while an artwork by Ray Saunderson brings contrasting color.

Gray walls in the older boy's bedroom are echoed in the furnishings and balanced by mustard-toned bedding.

OPPOSITE: Black and white mosaic marble floor tiles anchor a classic monochrome scheme in the ensuite.

The room shared by the younger boys features different shades of blue. Bronze strips on the shelves and cabinets, and pops of color in the artworks, provide detail and interest.

The rear of the house, with its manicured gardens and elegant pool, continues the layering of contemporary living over traditional style.

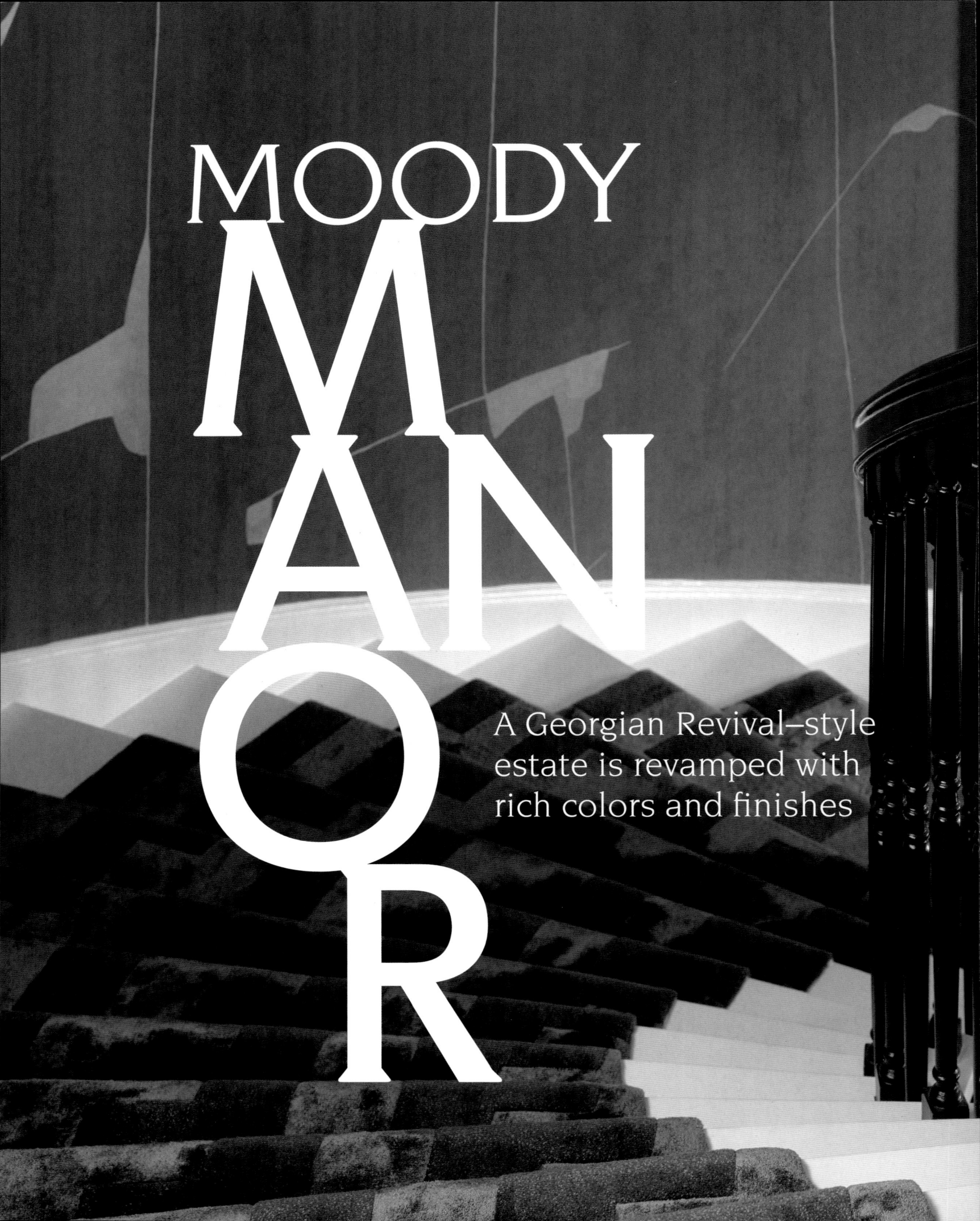

MOODY MANOR

A Georgian Revival–style estate is revamped with rich colors and finishes

Monochromes to moody burgundy. Painted walls to patterned wallpaper. Chandeliers that grow in size. Rooms that change purpose and color. It's natural that the style of a house undergoes different incarnations with the changing needs and tastes of its owners, and natural too that its interior layers evolve in response to this. What's unusual—and exhilarating—is being involved in all those incarnations, and having the chance to revisit and revamp a design that began ten years ago.

This was certainly the case with a grand two-story mansion in Melbourne. My relationship with the owners is itself layered with creativity. Since working with them on the first iteration of this place a decade earlier, I have also designed two country houses for them and their growing family, one in Australia and one in America, as well as a business headquarters in Victoria. I am very familiar with their style—I know they love deep heritage colors like burgundy, green, and blue, and that they prefer tonal blends to sharp contrasts. I also know how much they appreciate what layering brings to an interior, so when they approached me to redesign elements of their city home, I was keen to join them on this next evolution.

Built in the 1930s, the Georgian Revival–style building is expansive, with eight different living areas, inside and out, seven bedrooms, seven ensuites, and two powder rooms. Approaching the interior design afresh meant addressing new areas as well as reworking old ones to create a more complete, coherent setting in keeping with the owners' current lifestyle. It also allowed me to pursue some of the ideas I'd conceived from the beginning.

A generous reception room at the entrance was the biggest transformation. It was always a dramatic space, with square panels on its white ceiling, a white marble floor with black details, and charcoal stucco walls, but it wasn't being used enough. I had long envisaged its potential as a living room, and its proportions lent themselves beautifully to the symmetry of a formal layout. To bring more depth and drama to the room, I changed the floors to all-black marble and laid a black and charcoal moiré-patterned rug on top. On the walls, I introduced handpainted charcoal wallpaper with an irregular bronze thread running through it, which adds a shimmering metallic detail to the space.

The rug's border of burgundy and pink set the tone for the next level of layering, with burgundy curtains on the windows and doors. Hanging over sheer gold curtains, they visually draw ceiling and floor together to create a more intimate mood. The furniture presents inviting sculptural curves with two burgundy velvet vintage sofas and a brass and burl coffee table in between. Above, a five-foot-high chandelier of brass and crystal makes a strong statement that is balanced by the room's dimensions, and despite its size, the entire space appears lavishly furnished and welcoming.

Although the ceiling already featured a series of panels, I added several more moldings around the edges for extra detail. In fact, throughout the house, new ceiling moldings deliver an extra layer that is often enough to transform older rooms, while establishing a look that is more sympathetic to the era of the building.

Burgundy tones also bring a new layer to some of the old spaces. A patterned rug in the study deepens the palette of the room, enhanced by reupholstered mauve chairs that work beautifully with the timber shelves and charcoal stucco ceiling. In the casual living room, with its timber-slatted ceiling and wall of bookshelves, the color appears in various furnishings from an ottoman to vintage Murano lights, adding warmth to a new gray sofa. Those two shades continue in the kitchen opposite, where more vintage lights cast their delicate glow over burgundy leather stools, gray marble countertops, and gray-stained timber cabinetry.

In the dining area, the pink, gray, and burgundy hues of my rug anchor an elegant new furniture setting. The marble tabletop with its purple vein and the curved gray leather chairs echo the shape of the rug and that of the crystal chandelier, which was repurposed from the original entrance to enjoy its own new incarnation here.

On this floor, the newly decorated powder rooms were a chance to celebrate opulent layers of color and finish. In one, burgundy patterned wallpaper creates a richly hued space, with a custom lacquered vanity and velvet fringed bench further elevating the look. A pair of Pop artworks above the bench complete the effect, with a brass mirror, wall sconces, and vanity handles bringing a sophisticated gleam.

In the other powder room, across the original black-stained herringbone floorboards, a geometric patterned rug in gold, black, and gray echoes the brass details of a fluted glass screen. Custom mosaic tiles in the same colors as the rug connect to the gray marble vanity and timber cabinets beneath, while a gold-leaf mirror adds a strong decorative flourish.

On the upper floor of the house, I replaced the previous carpet of sharply contrasting black and white with a self-patterned carpet in two shades of gray. It stretches up the grand staircase and through the first-floor bedrooms, where a mix of updated old spaces and newly designed ones respond to the soft hues.

In the master bedroom, the gray tones of the existing charcoal silk wallpaper and taffeta curtains, the bedding, and paneled leather bedhead work with the carpet to create a calm, refined space against which bold abstract artworks bring splashes of color. The addition of pale pink cushions and a vintage bench reupholstered in pink and black velvet animal print soften the scheme and connect to a stunning pink leather sofa in the dressing room. A breakout area on the other side of the generous bedroom is an example of the house's layering over the years. What began with two teal velvet armchairs and a pair of metallic side tables and floor lamps now includes two brass coffee tables in bold organic shapes and a vintage sofa reupholstered in black velvet. New bookshelves edged in brass complete the setting in a room that is all about comfort and seclusion.

Ensuites were a chance to extend the palette of the bedrooms and play with luxe materials. The master ensuite embraces monochromes, with a graphite-toned fluted bath showcasing its form against black mosaic tiles and a gray marble floor. Brass wall sconces and frames on the fluted glass shower provide glamorous details. In one of the girls' ensuites, pretty rose marble tiles on the walls and floor continue the colors from her bedroom, where pink patterned grassweave wallpaper presents a delicate background to a blush velvet custom bed.

And then there are all the lively layers of the outdoor spaces, which begin with a chic al fresco living room in gray, green, and burgundy. Beyond this, with the vivid blue of the pool as inspiration, the owners wanted to create a European beach club vibe. In colors spanning navy to French blue, the patterned sofa, sun loungers, and day beds with their clusters of tables make a vibrant display against the house's red brick exterior.

Some of the rooms in this house appeared in my first book, where I began to explore the importance of layering in interiors. Since then, the family has grown and the house with it, and I look forward to witnessing their enjoyment of all the new layers—until, that is, the next incarnation.

A brass vintage lamp, a little greenery, and the vibrant colors of an armchair and a Dale Frank painting create a dynamic entry moment at the base of the stairs.

OPPOSITE: The grand facade of this Georgian Revival-style building offers a hint of what is to come.

A new rug and chairs reupholstered in mauve and burgundy refresh the study, enriching the warmth of the timber shelves. My custom-designed, art deco–inspired marble console (opposite) brings further materiality to the room, which features two artworks by John Olsen.

The former reception room is now a formal living room, with burgundy curtains and sofas lending a beautiful symmetry. A five-foot-high chandelier presides over my black and charcoal moiré-patterned rug to complete the setting.

Burgundy patterned wallpaper creates a dramatic finish in one powder room, enhanced by a custom lacquered vanity and brass accents.

OPPOSITE: A velvet fringed bench beneath Andy Warhol artworks adds to the room's sumptuous look.

Behind the dining setting on my Després rug, an artwork by John Olsen hangs on the gray silk wallpaper.

OPPOSITE: In the living room, a pair of vintage lamps and an existing cabinet relacquered in burgundy update the original furnishing scheme.

The pink frosted glass shade of a vintage lamp picks up the bold colors of an abstract artwork by Waldemar Kolbusz in the study area of the master bedroom.

OPPOSITE: The brass legs of a console deliver graceful lines beneath another Andy Warhol artwork.

A whimsical artwork by Anna Berezovskaya commands attention on the landing.

OPPOSITE: Handpainted Porter Teleo charcoal wallpaper with a bronze detail leads up the stairs to a dreamy Claire Kirkup artwork.

In the master ensuite, brass accents bring contrast to a graphite-toned fluted bath, gray marble floor, and black Bisazza wall tiles.

OPPOSITE: More Murano glass in a mirror by the entrance downstairs.

The gray palette of the master bedroom has been updated with the addition of a Waldemar Kolbusz artwork and a vintage bench reupholstered in pink animal print.

OPPOSITE: A pink leather de Sede sofa continues the color scheme, making a statement in the dressing room.

Teal velvet armchairs set the tone for the generous breakout area, which now also features brass coffee tables, a vintage black velvet sofa, Murano lamps, and new brass-edged bookshelves. An artwork by Martine Emdur adds its rich colors to the mix.

Geometric details and a palette of gold, black, and gray enliven another powder room.

OPPOSITE: Vintage lights bring a delicate balance to the gray marble countertops and gray-stained cabinetry in the kitchen, with burgundy leather chairs providing contrast.

Against the timber ceiling and bookshelves of the casual living room, touches of burgundy bring depth to the gray Minotti sofa.

Pink grassweave wallpaper and a custom blush velvet bedhead begin a layering of pink in one of the girls' rooms.

OPPOSITE: My Rubato tiles in Norwegian Rose marble continue the palette with their delicate details.

The vivid spectrum of blues in the outdoor furniture was inspired by the pool.

OPPOSITE: A new al fresco living room is a serene place to sit with its gray Minotti chairs and my Palazzo rug in green and burgundy.

The blue and white setting conjures up a European pool club vibe in the middle of Melbourne.

STEPPED STONE

Bespoke pieces and beautifully crafted materials bring the details in this striking home

Bold and precise, the concentric gray and white rectangles are a dramatic sight as they stretch out before you. On the ceiling, another series of powerful lines unfolds in textural white, drawing the eye further to invite you inside. The two create a dynamic display at the entrance of this vast contemporary residence, and yet there is not a patterned rug or wall covering in sight.

Here, layering is not about the patterns in furnishings or accessories, but rather the interest of materials, the appeal of texture, the richness of color. It lies in the crafting of details and the superior finishes that range from interior architecture to the curated display of bespoke pieces.

The owners of this three-story, five-bedroom house in the leafy Sydney suburb of Hunters Hill wanted a striking, luxurious design for them and their three teenage children. The couple are not particularly fans of pattern but they love marble, and the deep tones of Pietra Grey and gold-tinged white of Calacatta Oro that form the striped effect at the entrance bring a special sense of grandeur to various spaces across the house.

I conceived the idea of a concentric-shaped marble floor as a way of adding interest to the entrance and beginning to tame its generous proportions. With the same end in mind, I designed the stepped ceiling that rises to follow the house's curved roof, and finished it in stucco, along with the surrounding walls, to create a textural effect. Between the two surfaces, a curved staircase of gray marble seems to mirror the lines of the ceiling, while a concrete balustrade presents a seamless wave that ends in an exaggerated curl, offsetting all the surrounding angles.

Only a few custom pieces are required to complete the setting—a burgundy velvet bench seat, a brass console, and a brass, black oak, and marble-top table. The table's circular shape is echoed in the brass chandelier above, and its discs of brass and black oak repeat the striped look of the marble in a different form. Abstract artworks bring bold splashes of color to an area that speaks of style and luxury.

A sense of luxury defines the entire house, in the lavish use of materials as well as the tailored decor, layered in a palette of white, gray, gold, and navy. Across giant slabs of gray marble, the dining setting presents a sophisticated and considered grouping, with custom navy velvet chairs around a black–gray marble table. The soft gray rug below is more about texture and tone than pattern, leaving the grandest statements for the interior architecture. Large square panels on the white ceiling begin a motif that continues throughout the house, while a portal of gray marble elevates a sideboard arrangement sitting within its frame. On one wall, more eye-catching panels appear in a brass fireplace, the gleaming finish of which is picked up in brass light fittings and accessories.

The use of brass brings a crisp punctuation of line to the adjacent kitchen, with art deco–style brass and stainless steel trims traversing the white cabinetry. Aside from these, the only pattern comes courtesy of the intricate veins of the Calacatta Oro splashback and countertop, and the square ceiling panels, which feature here on a smaller scale. Navy leather stools provide the balancing color and another connection to the dining area behind.

Navy appears in a mix of custom and vintage pieces, such as the teaming of a Milo Baughman sofa with custom leather ottomans in the family room. A custom black sideboard and abstract artwork on one wall offer more dark tones, but otherwise the room is bathed in light from

The exterior gates of the house feature a pattern also used at the front door, in one of many stylistic links throughout.

A view of the entrance through the bronze front door, which is framed by art deco–style panels.

OPPOSITE: An artwork by Waldemar Kolbusz brings a splash of color above a custom brass console and vintage brass and Murano glass lamps.

More bold color at the entrance, courtesy of a Monika Dalek artwork and a custom burgundy velvet bench.

OPPOSITE: Above the lines of the marble floor, the staircase with its concrete balustrade delivers a dramatic curve.

Ceiling panels in the kitchen continue the motif from the dining area (opposite) on a smaller scale, while brass lines frame the cabinetry.

OPPOSITE: Custom navy velvet dining chairs create an elegant grouping against the backdrop of the brass-paneled fireplace.

Navy leather ottomans and velvet sofas in the family room, as well as leather chairs in a sitting area (opposite), are offset by the sheen of brass accents.

The study, featuring Antonia Mrljak artworks, presents a moody setting with ebony walls and navy ceiling paneling.

OPPOSITE: Pale pink swirls in the powder room wallpaper offer a subtly textural effect.

Between the curved balustrade and the stepped stucco ceiling on the upper floor, a sculpture, artwork, and custom mirror bring their own striking lines.

A gray marble fireplace makes another statement in the master bedroom, with an artwork by Josef Albers on the wall outside, behind a Dan Murphy sculpture.

OPPOSITE: Behind the bed, a shagreen leather-paneled wall presents a luxurious surface in a room full of exquisite finishes.

Brass trims, fixtures, and accessories highlight the gold veins of Calacatta Oro marble in the master ensuite.

The two dressing rooms are rich in finishes, from gold and white marble-effect wallpaper to ebony joinery and a gray marble portal.

A Gio Ponti mirror sits between decorative wall sconces in this ensuite.

OPPOSITE: Pink-painted walls and de Gournay wallpaper bring a dreamy element to the bedroom, highlighted by the art deco–style bed.

On the warm tones of my London rug, Milo Baughman bronze tables and gray seating offer a casual yet stylish setting.

OPPOSITE: Ceiling-mounted lights in the stucco panels make for a dramatic display in the lower dining area.

The gray granite bar is elevated by the addition of brass details and the bold colors of an artwork by Michael Gromm.

OPPOSITE: Burgundy velvet chairs introduce a deeper hue to the cellar.

Black and white ceramic tiles create strong stripes in the changing rooms by the pool (opposite).

Beautiful landscaped gardens bring the bespoke layer of crafting outdoors.

NEW BRUTALISM

Concrete and rosewood team with midcentury touches in a modernist house

My passion for layering doesn't detract from the fact that I am a modernist at heart. The functional beauty of structure and form, the raw purity of materials such as concrete and timber—these were among my first loves. The opportunity to use them in a new build, working as architect and interior designer, allowed me to explore the power of layering in a more minimalist setting.

I owe my rekindled love of modernism to one of the owners, who passed away soon after the house was completed. The story of a house is intimately linked with that of its people, and for me this one is imbued with emotion. An old friend and her husband wanted me to create a midcentury-inspired residence for them and their three children. Before she died, Michelle brought her vision to every aspect of the design, inspiring me to mix materials and colors, and to approach things with a fresh eye.

Knowing the couple wanted a house that featured concrete, timber, black brick, and patterned outdoor tiles, my thoughts went to the Brazilian brutalist style of modernist architect Paulo Mendes da Rocha. I have long admired the stark beauty of his designs in raw concrete, and the generosity of space that he evoked through the strong interplay of outdoor and indoor areas. The three-story, five-bedroom house is located on a cliff by the Georges River in southern Sydney, and I could see how this style would sit well amid the surrounding greenery and subtropical coastal outlook.

Concrete plays an important part in the layering of the house, taking on a decorative role beyond its structural significance. The exterior sets the tone for what follows inside, with off-form concrete slabs creating an attractive grid appearance that is enhanced by the tie holes visible in each block. These are filled with brass, producing a pattern of small gleaming discs that come into their own on the walls of the house's interior.

The use of concrete takes a more intricate turn on some of the ceilings, with formed beams creating a striking woven look above the stairwell and the long bridge that runs adjacent to it, connecting rooms on the upper floor. These two light-filled areas are central to the spirit of the design, in terms of their materiality and their link between indoors and outdoors. Here and throughout the house, huge windows offer views of the water beyond, while internal spaces look into one another, across different levels or filtered through fluted glass.

Below the woven-style concrete ceilings of the two spaces, floorboards of American walnut provide a textural finish, with blackened steel balustrades delivering a delicacy of line that maintains the open ambience of the house. The palette begins to make itself known here, with soft pink acting as the base note for a considered clash of colors. A pink glass and brass pendant hangs, jewel-like, over the stairs, while pink sheer curtains and painted cabinets flank the upstairs bridge. Across its timber floor, my art deco–style runner in red, pink, yellow, black, and gray captures the house's hues in a bold mix that almost vibrates with energy.

Blush pink was a favorite color of Michelle's, and her instinct for introducing it was a persuasive factor that helped to soften the various surrounding concrete surfaces, through elements such as a stucco wall at the entrance. In this area, the hue seems to gain warmth from ceilings of rosewood—a timber I introduced for its rich tropical appearance and ability to transition smoothly from inside to outside. The space is not overly layered, so pieces draw focus with their color and finish, such as the sculptural shape of a burgundy lacquered console.

Concrete and rosewood continue to make an impact in the open-plan kitchen, dining, and living areas on the floor below. In the kitchen, rosewood presents an eye-catching composition of forms that reflect Michelle's unique vision, with upper cabinets in an asymmetrical cubist-style design and, on the island, a veneer of hand-cut panels laid in a midcentury-inspired starburst pattern. Green leather stools introduce another color that has a strong presence throughout the house, appearing in the marble custom dining table and the pendant light, with burgundy dining chairs providing tonal balance.

That rich color combination anchors the lounge room, a large space that shares the open-plan area and its polished concrete flooring but feels like a separate zone due to a sunken floor. In a room where the layers are few but significant, a modular sofa in forest green acts as a framing device, with an integrated concrete ledge on the opposite wall completing the effect. Concrete delivers a decorative layer again via the ceiling, which features crisscross concrete beams across panels of rosewood. I designed the rug of burgundy, gray, and yellow to mirror the ceiling's diamond-patterned structure, and the two form an appealing shell that increases the room's intimacy without losing any of its modernity.

Rosewood brings earthiness and detail to the adults' study, in diagonal ceiling panels, a desk, and vintage shelves mounted on the black brick walls. On the same floor, the children's study displays a brighter palette, teaming white-painted brick with teal cabinets and bench seating in mismatched orange and mustard patterned fabrics.

The eclectic mix of colors and finishes resumes on the top floor of the house. In the master bedroom located here, Michelle encouraged me to introduce a timber ceiling painted in a French wash of teal, which contrasts dramatically with the burgundy velvet custom bed. To ensure a cohesive area, I continued the teal finish in the ensuite, where it brings a lighter look to the walls and timber ceiling. Here, too, another unexpected element driven by my friend is the black and white marble floor, laid in an irregular pattern.

The children's bedrooms offer uplifting moments of color through their layers of bedding, cabinetry, rugs, and curtains, while different bedheads give each its own personality. Their ensuites share the typography of small square wall and floor tiles, marble vanity countertops, and terrazzo basins in different colors. Some of that materiality plays out in the house's two powder rooms. Both have black marble vanities: one juxtaposes it with a pink terrazzo basin and walls of aged mirror, black brick, and concrete; the other with a wall of small black and white tiles, and rosewood accents. Their look remains modern but the mix of finishes surprises and delights.

If tiles bring a layer of interest to the bathrooms, they are the defining element of the outdoor terraces. Beyond the kitchen and dining areas, patterned floor tiles set the scene for outdoor entertaining beneath a dining setting of burgundy chairs. Outside the studies, the same tiles offset the citrus tones of the seating, the black brick walls, and the lush greens of the garden.

On the lowest floor, geometric patterned monochrome tiles connect the outdoor terrace to the bar area inside. A generous space, its rosewood ceiling features a coffer in concrete, which echoes the circular form of the teal velvet sofa and ottoman at its center—a piece that offers another rich clash of color and material with the burgundy marble bar behind it. Through floor-to-ceiling windows, this room enjoys an expanse of view that includes indoor and outdoor areas, and the stretch of water beyond.

In this way, interior and exterior spaces continue to interact against a robust blend of materials and colors. It is a stunning house that embraces Brazilian brutalism, interpreted through the lens of an Australian Italian modernist and inspired by a dear departed friend, whose passion and vision can be felt in every room and whom I am honored to have known.

The off-form concrete slabs and black bricks of the exterior create a strong contrast with the surrounding greenery.

At the entrance, beneath an artwork by Phoebe Halpin, a burgundy lacquered console picks up the pink tones of the rosewood ceiling and a nearby stucco wall.

OPPOSITE: A Paulistano chair by Paulo Mendes da Rocha sits at the end of my art deco–style runner on the bridge.

Rosewood accents and the owners' vintage light bring warmth to the monochrome scheme of the powder room.

OPPOSITE: The stairwell with its pink glass and brass pendant is a study in light and line.

In the sunken lounge room, the pattern of the rug mirrors that of the concrete beams on the ceiling. The sofa, vintage chair, and artwork by Sue Beyer bring more layers of color.

Behind the green marble-top dining table and burgundy chairs, a treasured custom mirror recalls the lines of architect Carlo Scarpa.

OPPOSITE Patterned concrete tiles complete the outdoor dining setting.

Black cabinetry, black granite benchtops, and a marble splashback with veins of red and purple contrast beautifully with the rosewood in the kitchen.

The adults' study pairs the finishes of rosewood and black brick with an artwork created by friends and family, adding a heartfelt touch. Vintage elements include a green Fritz Hansen chair and rosewood shelves.

Another outdoor terrace connects the studies, its seating adding a bold splash of color.

OPPOSITE: In the children's study, an eclectic mix of pattern and color creates a vibrant space.

A timber ceiling in a French wash of teal softens the master bedroom, where an iconic photograph by Helmut Newton sits above a custom burgundy bed.

OPPOSITE: Teal continues in the ensuite, which features a black and gray marble floor in a custom lay.

In this bedroom, steel blue cabinetry balances the warm tones of the vintage bedhead, the artwork by Morgan Stokes, and rug by Olsen + Ormandy from Designer Rugs.

OPPOSITE: White square ceramic tiles and a terrazzo basin give a bright and strongly defined look to the ensuite.

The stunning form of a vintage dressing table and mirror is a feature of this pink-toned bedroom.

OPPOSITE: The soft hues continue in the ensuite, with its pink ceramic tiles and terrazzo basin.

A second powder room introduces dramatic finishes, including a wall of aged mirror.

OPPOSITE: Artworks by Hayden Jackson feature in two of the bedrooms. Here, a custom teal velvet bed teams with pink tones.

A teal velvet Milo Baughman sofa forms the centerpiece of the downstairs bar area, its shape echoed in the ceiling coffer.

Vintage stools and Eames dining chairs bring midcentury touches to the burgundy marble bar, enhanced by custom walnut and rattan joinery nearby, housing a much-loved record collection (opposite).

From its waterfront exterior, the monumental structure of the house and its materials can be truly appreciated.

OPPOSITE: Even the mismatching colored sun loungers by the pool reflect the personality of one of the owners.

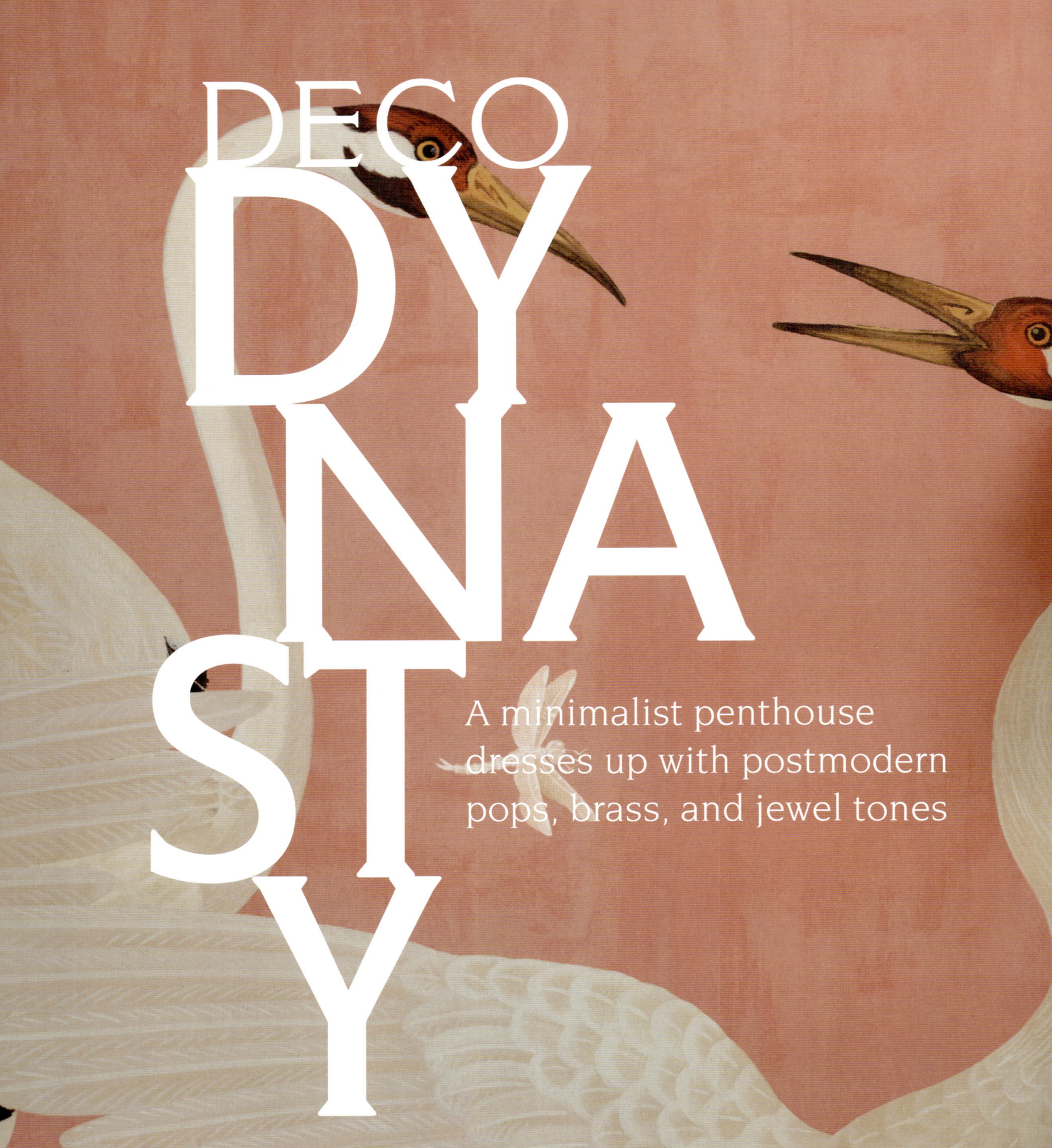

DECO DYNASTY

A minimalist penthouse dresses up with postmodern pops, brass, and jewel tones

There's something enticingly voyeuristic about looking inside other people's homes. Seeing how they live, their style, and the design choices they make offers us a glimpse of another world, and whether that world is real or fictional, it can offer rich inspiration. When I was young, the interior worlds I saw on television depicted a fascinating fantasy life that would eventually set me on my career path. Among the many set designs, the apartment of *Dynasty*'s fabulous villain Alexis Carrington made a great impression on me. White with pink and maroon accents, art deco touches, and an unmistakable air of Hollywood, it was a tribute to 1980s opulence.

Images of Alexis's apartment were certainly in my mind when I began the renovation and interior design for this three-bedroom penthouse in the trendy Melbourne suburb of Toorak. The owners, a lovely, glamorous young couple who run a luxury watch and jewelry business, wanted to turn their all-white minimalist space into a lavishly furnished home with a strong sense of grandeur. Both are fans of stylish jewel tones, particularly pink and maroon—they'd actually been inspired by the latter after seeing it painted on the walls of my Sydney apartment.

The process of layering extends as far back as the themes and inspirations for a design, and in this case there were a few. On top of that *Dynasty* vibe, the 1980s palette of pink and maroon over a white background led me to play with the colors and forms of postmodernism, which I embraced in designing various custom rugs for the apartment. A warm, textural, and luxurious layer in any interior, these rugs reference an art deco sensibility in their linework. Their unique patterns also assist in delineating different spaces throughout the apartment, an element that was missing from the open-plan layout.

The owners' choice of palette also coincided with a recent trip

I'd made to Paris. My mind was still filled with the sophisticated combination of maroon, burgundy, and brass that adorned everything from the interiors of cabarets and chic bars to the packaging of old-school perfume bottles. However, inspiration didn't just come from colors—the striking use of arches in French architecture was another idea I would draw on in creating grand statements for this home.

And then there was the wonderful Jonathan Adler. The owners possessed a collection of his furniture and wanted an interior designer who would be simpatico with his aesthetic. I love the color, wit, and ingenuity of shape present in Adler's designs, and I looked forward to incorporating them into the apartment's transformation.

Bringing all these elements together, I wanted to celebrate the owners' passion and profession, lifestyle and love of dressing up, arraying their pieces rather like jewels themselves on display for enjoying every day.

One of the great things about a minimalist white space is that it presents a blank canvas, and here I had the chance to layer the design from the walls themselves. The introduction of different sized arches was key to creating distinctive areas as well as making architectural statements. To build up a sense of entrance, I began with the corridor that led from the front door, installing two arches that give the space elegance and purpose. Mirrored panels along the walls of one and maroon-painted doors along the other deliver beautiful finishes, offset by gray wallpaper on the ceiling that has a stucco effect. With sculptural wall sconces and a striking runner in pink and gray tones, the space is dramatic and alluring, immediately establishing this as a special residence.

From here, you step into a world of lacquered walls, rosy hues, and warm brass touches, punctuated with black and white. This scheme comes into its own in the dining room, where you're greeted by a luxurious expanse of Gucci wallpaper, featuring delicate white herons against a pink background. Taking that color to the next level are Jonathan Adler dining chairs, which I reupholstered in ombré shades of velvet from orchid to burgundy. Brass makes an impact here in the brutalist forms of a Jonathan Adler credenza and the robust, organic lines of a brass dining table. A white and brass vintage light is a stunning centerpiece that forms part of the language of lighting in the apartment, which includes a range of vintage and contemporary pendants and wall sconces.

To separate the dining room from the living areas, I introduced another arch, integrating it into a larger structure covered in white lacquered fluting. The addition also hid a structural column, but with Paris still on my mind, I like to think of it as a little Arc de Triomphe moment. With its inner curve plated in brass, like the other arches throughout the apartment, it makes a beautiful statement without blocking the flow of the space. The fluting is a detailed cohesive device that covers most walls, its lacquered look adding to the apartment's luxe finishes. Tying all the spaces together further are the blush-painted ceilings and blond wood floors.

The living and sitting rooms offer different experiences defined by their furnishings. In the living room, a maroon velvet sofa is a plush foil for the maroon lacquered wall that sits behind a fireplace of Calacatta Viola marble. Between these, the organic forms of nesting tables, blush velvet chairs, and a contemporary pink quartz pendant light sit over a golden rug with lines that fan out like rays of sunshine.

In the adjacent sitting room, the mood is more playful but no less refined, with an acrylic and brass coffee table flanked by a pair of Jonathan Adler sofas. I reupholstered the sofas in a lively postmodern pattern that introduced teal, another jewel-like color.

To give the kitchen its own grand aspect, I framed it with an elongated arch featuring a flattened top. More Viola marble appears on the countertop of the white lacquered island, while fluffy white lambswool stools add a feminine touch. Together with the vintage-style pendant and the maroon lacquered joinery, these create a sleek space that is beautiful as well as functional.

The sumptuous nature of maroon brings its moody glamour to the master bedroom, with my self-patterned wallpaper that gives a sultry, textural feel to the room. The effect is heightened by the addition of an eye-catching four-poster bed in an antiqued gold finish, with gold-toned bed furnishings making this a deliciously decadent retreat. A piece of furniture in maroon lacquered fluting that sits at the foot of the bed cleverly hides a pop-up television, while glossy maroon doors lead to the adjacent ensuite and dressing rooms.

After the deeper hues of the bedroom, the ensuite presents a lighter palette of black, white, and gray in patterned mosaic tiles from Bisazza. I chose a chain-link pattern as a playful reference to the owners' profession—stretching from floor to ceiling, the tiles bring a change of pace but still speak of luxury. Further indulgence awaits with two dressing rooms, one surrounded by mirrored cabinets that make it appear like a modern Versailles boudoir.

But guests, too, are given the star treatment, with a bedroom cocooned in soft pink wallpaper, and a powder room that marries the burgundy ripples of a Viola marble vanity with the rich merlot of Pierre Frey marble-effect wallpaper. Like the apartment itself, clad in the well-dressed sheen of white lacquer, these spaces envelop and enrich with their layers of color, pattern, and finessed finishes. I'd like to think that if Alexis herself came to visit, she'd feel right at home in this urban jewel.

An arched corridor featuring mirrored panels, sculptural lights by Kelly Wearstler, and my custom runner creates a real sense of entrance.

OPPOSITE: White lacquered fluting and brass accents are among the apartment's luxe finishes. The arched structure makes a grand statement while dividing the dining room from the living areas.

A pair of reupholstered Jonathan Adler sofas and my custom rug combine postmodern forms with a palette of pink, maroon, and teal in the sitting room for a lively look.

OPPOSITE: A brutalist-style credenza makes an impact before a background of pink Gucci wallpaper.

The kitchen, framed by an elongated arch, features a wall of lacquered maroon joinery hiding a generous scullery behind.

OPPOSITE: Maroon tones continue in the living room, where a pendant light by Christopher Boots is the crowning jewel.

My Appia wallpaper in maroon sets the scene for sultry glamour in the master bedroom, which features an artwork by Julie Hutchings.

OPPOSITE: Mosaic tiles in a jewelry-inspired chain-link pattern give a playful personal touch to the ensuite. The glossy door and vintage lights provide the pops of color in this monochrome scheme.

The rich hues and patterns of the marble vanity and marble-effect wallpaper create a decadent enveloping effect in the powder room.

OPPOSITE: The palette and design of my custom rug and the maroon ottoman create a kaleidoscope of color in the mirrored dressing room.

ACKNOWLEDGMENTS

There are many people I want to thank, whose devotion, skills, and hard work have helped make this book a reality.

Thank you to my dedicated team of staff—everything we create is a group effort and I couldn't do it without you: Renee Alam, Matia Bassi, George Berry, Lisa Dingelmaier, Vanessa Giampietro, Anna Girardi, Blaize Goodwin, Jess Hill, Georga Huntriss, Connie Lia, Mary Papantoniou, Tom Phu, Adam Pierpoint, Doris Sawires, Natalie Timmins, and Victor Wong.

To my book team, thank you for your support, vision, and patience: Anna Viniero, my hard-working art director and best friend of thirty years; Fiona Daniels, a true talent with words who has helped shape each of my books; Georgie Frew, whose enthusiasm and positivity keep us all buoyed up; Anson Smart and Russell Horton, who have been photographing my projects so beautifully for fifteen years; and Daniel Melamud at Rizzoli, who has guided and supported me through two books now. Thank you also to Claud Cecil Gurney for his kind words in the foreword.

And thanks to Tiana Webb-Evans for mentoring and inspiring me on this next stage of my design journey.

To my incredible clients for letting me express my creativity and gifting me with your trust, thank you: Leticia Francini and Steven Ninnes, Bella Li, Angela and Chris Antoniou, Rosanna and Joseph, Michelle and Zack Sotiropoulos, Jaimee and James Kennedy, and those who wish to remain private.

Thanks to my other collaborators: Ben Avery, Bisazza, Melissa and Vince Ciolino, Elliott Clarke, Conley & Co, Claire Delmar, Carmelo and Luigi Ginardi, Evan Manolio, Mark Mastronianni, Robert Murdocca, Signature Prints, RJA, Designer Rugs, Corey Stone, Teranova, and Theo Glekas and Nick Tsaousidis.

Thank you to Curatorial+Co., Flinders Lane Gallery, .M Contemporary, Nanda\Hobbs, Olsen Gallery, Studio Gallery, the Art and Framing Company, Traffic Jam Galleries, and Wentworth Galleries.

And finally, a big thank you to my partner of sixteen years, Jason Greenhalgh, who helps me continue to create all my crazy dreams and lives them with me every day.

This book is dedicated to my dear friend Michelle, who passed away during its production. I was privileged to know Michelle for nearly thirty years and honored to have a role in creating her dream house, which features in these pages. With her passion for life and down-to-earth nature, she challenged me to push myself and reawakened my love of modernism. Her memory will continue to inspire me.

MICHELLE SOTIROPOULOS
1972–2021

First published in the United States of America in 2022
by Rizzoli International Publications, Inc.
300 Park Avenue South
New York, NY 10010
www.rizzoliusa.com

Photography: Anson Smart
Credits: p.8: Sam Francis work of art
© Sam Francis. Artists Rights Society [ARS]/Copyright Agency, 2022
pp.168, 169, 174: John Olsen works of art
© John Olsen/Copyright Agency, 2022
pp.173, 176, 177: Andy Warhol works of art
© Andy Warhol Foundation for the Visual Arts, Inc. ARS/Copyright Agency, 2022
p.216: Josef Albers work of art
© Josef Albers. VG Bild-Kunst/Copyright Agency, 2022

Text: © 2022 Greg Natale & Fiona Daniels
Foreword: © 2022 Claud Cecil Gurney
Editor: Daniel Melamud
Proofreader: Megan Conway
Production: Barbara Sadick
Design & Art Direction: Anna Viniero

All rights reserved. No part of this publication may be reproduced, stored in a retrieval system, or transmitted in any form or by any means, electronic, mechanical, photocopying, recording, or otherwise, without prior consent of the publisher.

Library of Congress Control Number: 2022930007
ISBN-13: 9780847872091

2022 2023 2024 2025 / 10 9 8 7 6 5 4 3 2 1

Printed in China